From Menopause to Zen-o-pause

Kyan Howland R.N. M.A.

Author of Wake the Mermaid

Balboa Press books may be ordered through booksellers or by contacting:

Balboa Press
A Division of Hay House
1663 Liberty Drive
Bloomington, IN 47403
www.balboapress.com
1 (877) 407-4847

Interior Image Credit: Kyan Howland

ISBN: 978-1-9822-5092-8 (sc)
ISBN: 978-1-9822-5093-5 (e)

Print information available on the last page.

Balboa Press rev. date: 07/22/2020

A DIVISION OF HAY HOUSE

for Georgia O'Keeffe

who believed in flowers even in the desert
and painted them powerfully, as if they're mountains or woman.

who said these three~

~Imagination makes you see all sorts of things.

~Fill a space in a beautiful way.

~I feel there is something unexplored about woman that only a woman can explore.

~One~

The questions one asks in menopause are many and maddening~

*just how big are my breasts going to get
*why did I just wake for the ninth time
*will I drown from these night sweats
*why did I marry him/her
*should I try a matcha coconut latte
*when will this rollercoaster of emotion end
*why is this headache the size of grandma's casserole
*where did those thirty pounds come from when I didn't even eat the cheesecake
*is that enough water, because my belly goes glug
*why does it feel like my life is both over and yet never-ending with fatigue

Love, the angst of menopause is real.
You feel like a jellyroll hit by a milk truck.

And that uterus. Overachiever!
Doing a Houdini, putting you in knots and a dark place.

Please know dearest, your humor, honesty, and creative response
are your best tri-force and can change the day with its kiss.

Breathing room is yours. Read on.
I believe we can feel more beautiful than a flower
despite the insane pain, crazy town moods, hot flashes,
mad dashes to the store for chocolate, and the sea of tears.

Menopause is magnificent
in a sick sort of urban legend way. Here's why.

You no longer have red like a monthly stop sign on the corner.
It means, go, though you're no longer on any road you know.
And while sometimes, on this empty road,

it's like a horror movie with Santa suddenly back
in red, during summer vacation,
you can laugh as it devastates
as you wait for the present. The present!

Life is art, more than ever.

If you choose the art of self-care and awareness,
menopause will slip into a place I call zen-o-pause.
Imagine that!

Make space for a change involving blood and love.
Innovate from the ground up. Get that authentic.

Thanks to those drama queens progesterone and estrogen,
you're part of production "Wicked".

Menopause! Who came up with that name
mentioning men? I'm tired of defining
myself by things outside me. Men, jobs, religion, and country.

I simply want to be me, a woman pausing,
stretching, making room for myself. As I am.
Oh, to meander at my own pace between moon and sun.
Getting it done, without having to try.

Menopause has come to mean
I don't press myself small to appease the male ego
or go to any event I don't care about.
And I've long set down the diaper bag and snacks,
so I can saunter as if I have all the time in the world.
I'm an ancient child once again talking to trees
wanting to understand rooted flight.

Lately, when I feel lost,
I return in my imagination to kindergarten.
I go to that cozy room where there's a nap matte.
The pretend kitchen is by a big window
where I talk to birds researching pie recipes.
Work is play. I enjoy saying ok, no, maybe, grrr.

I remember being asked to be a flower in a production
but refusing, because I wanted to be the rain.
Jumping off the chair
and waving my hands in the air was razzmatazz.
At the time, softly blooming was not where it was at.

Today, I'm longing to go softly, with ease and beauty.
But a storm started in my forties.
My hormones sent repeated red memos and
demanded
I slow down and show up as I am.

And so entropy takes me with a mad embrace,
as I face the crypt keeper each morning.

Some days I cry because it's so strange and hard.
Skin and hair fall off like petals.
It's as if I'm disappearing.

I'm here, but where is that?

Modern culture tells the woman over fifty
your life is winding down. Over!
They say this over and over.
They say lovers will leave you for
someone younger with a slip and slide.

Yet, freedom from their expectations is intoxicating.
Freedom from the male gaze! Yazzz.
No more performance, just spontaneity,
as I let go of what the world expects of me,
as I come as I am. Authentic.
Leaping off chairs as the tempest,
then pausing as a flower on the floor
as I root for me. I get down in the mud and blood,
lost in wonder,
appreciating how much I've come through.

My Grandma Dorothy Ella Henrietta used to say
if I do say so myself this is good
after making gravy, and now I understand.
I'm here to be where I am and say I feel good,
to announce it, whether anyone listens or not.

I feel good. Yes, even in menopause.
I feel awe, not just the awful
told and sold me.

Because you know what?
There's treasure tucked in menopause.
A secret peace where suddenly you're happy,
because you realize much you thought mattered, doesn't.

And you have no time for worry or complaint or tizzies.
You're busy being happy. Awestruck.
Opening the door with ohhh rather than oh-oh.

Announcing to the world, I feel goooooood!

And then going out in to the world
as a badass advocate for the sake of happiness and the planet.

So here you are, asking what's next
as menopause hits with its 7.1 quake.

Things we kept, collected, and slept with
break, leave, change.

It's truly a new day and menopause
is here not only to devastate but to
orchestrate happiness.
Yes, I said that. As you're shaken to your
core as more falls away, let it. Make a
f*cket and a bucket list.

Glimpse what's possible, now that the
bleeding has given way to….this place
of strange happiness, where cramps
stampede like red horses to remind you
of an adventure, get ready for more!

Menopause arrives to give your life back
after dispersing it in a million drops over
decades.

And while life is anything but neat and nice, you
wouldn't want it any other way.
Your quest should you accept it is to rest in the midst of
physiological protest.
To make it through another day of menopause with its
sleep deprivation, angst, and built-in-sauna.
Yes you'll have to be a ninja and bungee jump the drop
of estrogen.
You get to eat super foods you never have. Kale chips!
And after graduating from the Yale of kale,
you bravely take on chickpeas and edaname.

Taken to an edge, again and again
of mood, madness, food, and libido,
your heart beats fast for no reason.
You're either about to die or feel more beautifully alive.

Don't judge, just continue.

Remember the years when you prayed the blood would
come, because you didn't want to be pregnant?
Suddenly, you could find yourself wanting to hold a
baby and burst into tears.
You'd risk your life to time travel if you could.
You bloat as if pregnant. But you're not.
A dryness in your vagina feels like grief.
And you ache from deep inside your lips and legs
as the possibility of this, leaves.

Yes, a sense of dread and apprehension
makes it hard to concentrate.
Yet, it's easier to see through people and situations with
intuition, which makes life even more interesting.
You break through

from the place where you felt in control, to a wholeness
where you sing beneath the moon.
And you talk to ancestors, as if you're on a mysterious
ley line, while walking the hallway in your slippers.

The punk band 'blood' has kicked you out.
Will you still sing, say your say, and stay hot?

Next, it's as if you're invited to an all night rave in the
art district. You're disoriented, invigorated, afraid,
and can't sleep and arrange the furniture at midnight
listening to Fado.

Life is unrecognizable
with the impending sense that it's time. Time for what?
Ten, nine, eight…
let the heat propel you through space and time to
find out.
Be a menopausal astronaut, defy your own gravity.

I remember when life felt especially heavy.
I bled every two weeks for months.
I grew anemic and had cramps worse than anything
as a teen. It had me thinking I needed a hysterectomy.
Instead, I went on a road trip, heading west.
My first vacation in six years.
Being a single mom and making a living
had asked everything of me.

I was turning fifty and said that's it. I'm going.
I don't care how much blood is flowing.
I went to the desert which really made no sense.
Made a deal with myself that if I still feel weak
from blood loss, I'd have the surgery.

Perhaps, my body heard or maybe I tuned in more
deeply as I did yoga in the desert.
Zen acceptance swept over me
as I sweat and wept in over one hundred degree heat.

Bhakti fest was for four days. I admit, I stayed at the
air-conditioned hotel for the first two days
getting much needed R and R.

Then, I went with my heat, into the heat.
Like a desert rose, I opened to messages on every level.

Menopause is honest.
It reveals much with its heat, as you dare to pause,
listen, cry, decode, and know yourself as if for the first
time.
I forgave myself and felt grief over my divorce years
before.
I glimpsed a time when my daughters would grow up
and leave.
I wondered about love, about so much I loved and lost
and still loved.
I wondered about my dream to finish a book called
Wake the Mermaid.
(twenty years of research, which I just finished!)

I felt peace as I bled and wept in the desert sand.

During one group meditation, I stared into the eyes of
another woman lost in the gaze of the
white Tara. As we simply looked in each other's eyes,
differences disappeared, boundaries melted, the
universe turned inside out.

I felt pain melt away as I detached from my story and
simply breathed
and released who I am, which paradoxically helped me
receive who I am.

It was then I knew I'd be ok.
I stopped fighting menopause subconsciously.
Went home. The every two week bleeding stopped.
I didn't need surgery.

And that autumn, I fell madly in love for the first
time in years.

Menopause transmuted to zen-o-pause.
I accepted myself like I never had.
Laughed. Made music.
Walked in the rain. Had migraines. Made love.
Bled ever so often.

Made promises of a forever love which ended a year later.

And then, four more years of hot flashes and fatigue
as scaffolding added itself to my belly.

A sadness asked me to be alone and soon I was alone
in a way I'd never been before, ever.
Both my daughters came of age and moved away
just after their father died of pancreatic cancer.
And then, the pandemic hit. I worked as a nurse and got sick.
Took stock of what I want and wrote this book.
And now I'm in this abyss of having three months without work
without anyone else to care for. I pause. Face an abyss.

Nietzsche said "And when you look long into an abyss, the abyss also looks into you"

Pausing by this abyss, I feel the day as my soulmate.

Yes, menopause is a pause from men
but so much more.
It's a mysterious hello as you go into a dark room
where the top three priorities are~
keep going
eat dark chocolate
leave the light on for yourself.

That last one may ask you to be bioluminescent. So.
Get lit.

Notice your eyes blaze as you gaze in the mirror
in your loneliest moment. You are loved even as you
are undone.

Virginia Woolf once said, a woman needs "a room of
one's own."

I now have a body of my own,
free of pregnancy and bleeding.

Teutonic plates shift as we speak.
I make a grilled cheese
just for me, not for a crew. It's not that I don't love
others, but it's time to love me too.
Do you understand this kind of self-kindness?
Passion, rather than the rational, decided this.
I relax and remember who I am.

I'm an island, surfacing
from the heat my body makes.
I'm Hawaii thanks to my hormones.

I am something I didn't intend to become.

I didn't choose this tumultuous passage.
But today I choose to be tenacious and amazing.
Wise and kind. Angry and forgiving.

A maven in menopause
who instinctively knows
how not to bleed,
but who now has a heat index
that creates a new world.
A cuntry, unmapped and passionate.

Catapulted into a world I don't understand, I feel invincible in my vulnerability at unexpected moments.

Having survived the first time I bled, I sense I'll survive the last.

Remember the shame you may've felt as you bled just before the dance, afraid it would seep through your lavender dress?

Somehow, we got through the fear of pregnancy, the abortion, the miscarriage, the first birth of our child, the third. We persevered and proceeded through life, traveling at the speed of blood.

Visceral. Divine. Daring. Caring too much for others sometimes while not caring enough for ourselves.

And here we are today, taking ourselves off the shelf.
Women half a century old. Bold. In a new now.

The dew of tears on our cheek, as we look west believing the best is yet to come.

And so we go, into the beautiful.
Fully, freely, deeply.
Pause with awe, despite what's awful about menopause.
Life is always difficult and magnificent, simultaneously.

We vacillate between war council and candlelit bath.
We hone with a haiku focus and don't have time for complicated b.s.
We don't give a damn about anything, except what we love,
which is topped off with a nap and cat.

~**Two**~

Enough is enough.

But is it enough? TBD.

Time to roll up the red carpet
and get to it.

I'm well on my way.

Truly. Sa ta na ma.

I've let a lot go, at this point.
Kids. Partners. Jobs. Dreams.
Since I parted with pads,
tampons, and diva cups, I have
room on the shelf for more
books and chocolate.

And now this red friend no
longer arrives every month with
a sense of humor. This intimate
visitor has gone missing and I
miss it, even when not on time,
there was a familiarity.

So, what's left? Self-respect,
relentless self-love, time to
nap, and the space to wake
something else.

I notice I don't care about a lot
I once cared for. I believe I'll
never care at my own expense,
anymore.
I'm no martyr and my bleeding
wasn't punishment or the fall of
mankind. I am knowledge in
my body and won't apologize
for it.

The need for approval has been
removed. And a love of life
remains, as I make my way.

I fight to love rather than love to fight.
What a difference.
Maybe the fatigue I feel, is because I'm healing and simply need
to breathe, dream, wake, and take my time.

And those things I said I had to do,
which I maybe did or didn't
are a part of what I forget.
I believe even as I forget,
I remember to love the life I have,
as if for the first time.
Moving from *am*nesia to a place where I simply say I *am,*
has me bask in the everyday pleasure of sunshine on my skin.

Pausing to feel the kindness of being alive today
is what I'm here for. So, if I forget why I went to the cupboard
please understand, I'm remembering I love my life.

Zen-o-pause.
Is it possible? Keep open to how it centers you
when you're sad and befuddled.

You get to choose how you see menopause.
Do you resist or give a shift?

Even now, despite menopause, I know a gem is mine.
GEM~goddess empowered magnificence.

What say you, to taking on today!
Say hey, *I'm your champion*
I'm here for treasure, for all of it.

Give yourself the hour
as if it's a rare flower.

The greatest lesson ever on earth
is if you let yourself love and be loved.

To open, asks everything.
No judgement. Just love.

Sometimes a threshold doesn't
need a door for you to go through
to another world.

As you take your time to connect
to the sublime, you'll be less
addicted and fill with inspiration,
as you break through.

Slow down to remember who
you are and celebrate menopause,
with imagination and passion. As
you savor rather than save, the
ordinary becomes extraordinary.

Sometimes, I sing in my best
Marlene Dietrich voice "Lazy
Afternoon"

as I imagine daisies running riot,
as I relax on a hill of pillows.

Yes, let the rest fall away as you
rest
and the next thing you know,
life becomes music, despite
menopause. And possibly
because of it.

You arrive like a daisy, to live a
prolific politic.

Suddenly, you're the natural
woman Aretha sang about.
You're 'building a mystery' as
Sarah whisper sings.
You're 'feeling good' as Nina croons.
You're declaring 'all I want' as Joni
the poet and painter strums,
and screaming 'hey….what's going
on" with Four Non-Blondes.

There's quite a song list for
menopause, as you live life to the
hilt.
You know this to be true. Music
sees you through like nothing else.
The passionate crescendo of
menopause through your body
allows you to follow a flow, down
to every cell of your soul.
Again and again, you feel
fibonacci mystique
and make your way in a non-
linear, ancient ley line cycle.
As you transcend what seems like
the end,
you find yourself laughing and
beginning again,
rising to the wide blue sky.

Hot-flashing from the ashes.

Decolonized from domination at this time.
Beyond control in a tenacious state of creation.
You had no idea it'd be like this.
Society told you otherwise. But you're finding life, so fly.

Hot-flashing from the ashes.

And as you collaborate, connect, and create,
with this heat, you travel at the speed of light.
No longer concerned about being late,
you find a timing that organically opens.

If you and I are to go the distance,
we must make it sustainable.
As we bleed, need, and no longer
bleed, we greet a mystery.
We get a chance to accept mess.
To dance. To hold without
controlling.
As we do this, we're freed from
obsessive productivity
to achieve a feeling of worth just
from breathing,
just from being who and where
we are.

Here. Where flowers grow in our
soul, we glow in moonlight
of what was, is, and will be.

Rising, whimsical and wise.

For centuries, the female body has been subjugated and ignored.

Being present to menopause opens a portal
to travel past pain, shame, and oppression.

Make your way through trauma
Discover self-love.
Glisten!
Waste no time for superficial states of nice or cute.
Anything resembling fake flowers or brimming with yellow dye number 5
is far from real and won't satisfy. Be wild with your joy, your voice.

Live with verve. Curious about the world.

I remember the day I found my 'g' spot and that "g"
changed theories of sin to sing!

Be free from the need for approval and arrive at another level of freedom.
Free from self-sacrifice and definitions given to you in plastic wrap.

Admit honestly, you are *huge beauty*.

No more denying the power given
us by the sun.
The heat is creative. Mystic.
Travel past what they said wasn't
possible to where a moment
becomes a rose.

Gertrude Stein said "a rose is a rose
is a rose."

For a time, blood was a rose.
Incredibly, every month. You said
hi and goodbye to pleasure and
babies, making life bloom.

~Three~

They say your flow ceases, when
you stop bleeding.
So why do I feel so flow?

I find flow is no longer made of time
but of fire.

Menopause is a fire that doesn't
burn or consume,
but continues with unusual
beauty. We phoenix
from the ash of what was. They
call it hot flashing.

Extravagant. Empowered to strike
at life with hot magic.

We rise with heat, no longer
needing to bleed.

For decades, moon medicine
cooled you and I,
month after month. We were
earth, with our blood.
Now, we are birds who soar and
sear the sky.

The heat at the earth's core
found a door in us
and with this power, we create,
advocate, and face
the 1% who control 80% of the
world's wealth.

You, who bled without dying,
rise undeterred.
Unapologetic for your magic,
make today amazing.
Unleash a win/win/win for you,
others, and the earth.

No longer second-guess the
passion you have.
Believe in a collaboration where
you don't have to sacrifice
yourself.
You do not have to be nice and
negate your truth.
Instead, heal, lead, and feel the
music you are.

Sing like a siren calling out
above the sirens on the street.

Champion the moment. Then, another.
Authenticate. Author your life.

You're neither sweet biscuit nor ass-kicking bitch.
You're a lover, coming in to your power.

In this present form, you're neither repurposed, nor done.
No one can ignore you anymore, you're here. Lit.

Resplendent with menopause.

Burning serene.

A self-appointed priestess.
Instinctual.
Relentless.
Breaking beautiful.

Have mad respect for that.

Demand the revolution fill with revelation.
You who moved from ovulation to opulence,
teach how peace is possible.

For years you bled without wounding anyone.
Your conjured life with love and blood.

Once rich with the witchery to make a child,
you're filled with great tenderness to care for yourself.

Make room for all you are.

Bloom. Lift your head.

Mesmerize. Rise.

Realize how incredible it is.

Such sensual intelligence.

A radiance made of a whole
lifetime, shines inside you today.

Menopause asks for
an honest happiness
that can accomplish more than
any government.

Take time to breathe.

Flower powerfully.

Be this beautiful.

Express, experience, and exhale.
Let your belly goddess-relax and
laugh hard.

Go farther with your heart,
farther than you ever have.
And tell those who abuse power,
you're not having it.
Go out the door, to create a day.
Make sh*ft happen.

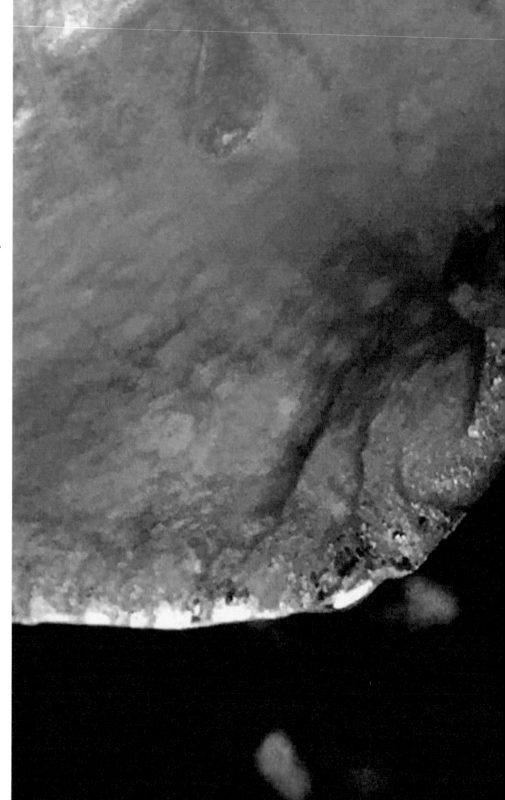

Sometimes, in the middle of the night

I feel like I'm an island. In the wake. Whole. Floating.
I don't feel alone. I actually feel more connected.

Like an island, I touch the flow of waves and a glow in the air.
I'm aware how my life is a part of everything. As if in a Vincent painting.

Few speak of this or dare to feel the depth of menopause.
They laugh, make a cliche out of it, and say you're just getting old.
But if you uncover the invitation to live more passionate,
you'll feel better and unf*ck the world a bit more.

Breath will be medicine. The sun, love.
Laughter and dancing, a part of your heart's rhythm.

Heat will be the creativity you learn to live from.

Wicked with inspiration
you'll find ways to brave every day like a quest.

This mythic place reveals a secret lagoon within,
where you belong in the midst of all you long for.
Feel craving fade into savoring, as you tune in to you.
A rare satisfaction spills into the day and leaves your heart singing.

Have passion and imagination. Explore everything
with a *joie de vivre*. Find zen-o-pause in menopause.

When insomnia comes, don't fight it. Go the party
thrown by those boisterous hormones. Toast two a.m.
Be a poet of all you know and don't know.
Raise a glass, a looking glass!
Look at life anew through a late night lens of zen.
Face the job you hate. Understand the guilt you took on
where you berated yourself for being late, convinced you came up short.
There's no more need to sacrifice yourself by being nice
or well-behaved or tame. There's only this raucous place
where your face is caressed by moonlight.

And here, where it's dark, one can't tell gender,
race, class, or age. You're simply here breathing,
burning, and turning another page.

Once, a doctor told me there's little I can do for menopause
but make lists. At the time, this frustrated me.
I forget to make lists. I wanted more help
and ended up finding incredible care from Dr. Rose Kumar,
author of the book Becoming Real. She addresses menopause
on every level. When we met, I felt heard. She taught me how to
reclaim health and feel better than ever.

I realized life does require a list but not the one I thought.
It's not about remembering what I had to do,
but who I still need to be.
In order to do this, I began making bliss lists!
Whatever delighted me during the day became the list.
As I came to my senses, I felt a revery and relief
seeing, tasting, touching, smelling, hearing, holding, and noticing my life.

Journaling my journey in the middle of the night
when I couldn't sleep, gave me a feeling of completeness,
as I realized how fully I alive I still am. I also made another list
of forgiveness. The dark stirs with secrets, regrets, and stories.
Get them out. Set them down. Turn the page.

Close your eyes. Open your heart.

I feel so free these days. Free of expectation. Free from my own crushing self-judgement. Saying I am this! Doing what Walt Whitman said "I celebrate myself, and sing myself" and feeling a new beautiful power.

Experience and expression are the unique truth we're given with every breath as we move through the universe, with as much love as we allow. So don't waste time being nice. Be kind. There's a difference. Compulsive niceness leads to dead ends, addiction, and people-pleasing. Menopause is a place to pause from people-pleasing, to meet yourself more deeply and truly.

And in the blue light from the refrigerator at three a.m. realize you're hungry for more than pizza.

You and I are way past doing, just to do it. Staying busy doesn't cut it unless it comes from our core. And there's more. It's not just what we do, but how we do it. Is it with passion and imagination?

No more 'trying'. Just do what you do the way you do it.

Don't let yourself be packaged as cliche, a woman doing menopause.

Shape shift. If you gain weight, don't criticize.
Let breasts and belly do their best Venus of Willendorf.
There's no perfect size. As long as you feel good, it's good.

When skin gets dry tell yourself its mermaid scales and treat yourself to a massage.

There's no time to waste with self-criticism.

You can't be mapped and won't be trapped between canyon and cloud.
Say *I'm the cosmos they call menopause.*

Recognize the entire spectrum of rainbow energy
shooting through the spine with hot *flashes*,
is how you rise from the ashes.

Much is changing. Why not take down false
constructs in civilization while you're at it.
Say yes, no. Enough!
Not now. Enough. Now.

Ever notice when you read 'now' backwards,
the word 'won' appears?

Come from this oneness.
Wake justice and joy in this place.
Deconstruct reality. Trust each beat of your heart
beneath the sky, beside one another, and the earth.

Let the earth teach you empathy.
The interconnection necessary to be healthy is here,
surfacing
as you trust even the suffering to teach you love.

Live by heart.
Respect the interconnection
necessary for yourself and others to be
safe and loved.

Follow the flow and glow, which is your real power.

Don't let anyone bulldoze your soul.

Menopause can become a field where we play
and say the craziest stuff.
As we remove layers of shame

and lay pain on the ground, it composts, becomes
something else.
Women once bled directly into the earth.
They gathered in sacred places to feel the power of
their cycle.

Let your words turn to birds
and your love to butterflies.
What would life look like,
if we prioritized community
more than consumption.
Creativity instead of competition.
Would forests still be pillaged, people violated,
the sea polluted, and the land raped toward rapid
extinction?

In a time that spends a billion each day on war,
it's more important than ever to take a nap
on a blanket, beneath the wide blue sky,
beside butterflies and laughing children.
Protect the authenticity of this with every breath.

Sing into existence the world you want,
like a goddess of old.
Go beyond the limits of what they say exists.

Now that you don't ink your panties, tell another
story, one without blood.

Your body is art and teaches you to be
creative. Live large.
Sculpt with a single gaze.
Rather than overanalyze, be amazed.

Come into your power even more and say *enough*.
Speak it with all your heart. Feel free.

Connect. Regenerate. Reach the enigma
where you're happy and sad. Lost and found.

Einstein the mystery of your experience.

Grieve. Feel relief.
Breathe and feel alive, from the core.

Love yourself and the world to the stars.
Go far into the dark and scintillate.

Shine with what's inside.

The fire you feel, burns, instead of bleeds.
Gifts you with real healing.

And because you bled for decades
without being wounded
or wounding someone, you know how to lead
without blame, rape, exploitation, or indifference.

Throw down your love with both arms.

Believe in a world where an inherent order
invites peace and creativity in daily life.
No armies needed.

Appease no one's ego, yours nor mine.
Realize someone's disapproval of you,
is about the other person
and has nothing to do with you.

Unusual creativity beats and breaks through
you now.
K'pow it to a new economy, healthcare paradigm,
and authentic politic.

Become something else now,
which the world is waiting for.
What you'll give the world from this moment on is
something phenomenal.

Zen-o-pause gets you from edge to center.

Hormones wake and take
you places you've never been.
Shorelines change.
The ebb and flow of estrogen
and progesterone ask everything.
It's as if you're pregnant all over
again, only this time you birth
yourself.

And it takes a lot to navigate the
intensity that has you collapse
on the couch and
build a pillow cocoon.
Menopause is both
metamorphosis and meditation.

The passion of it has you
shimmer with heat and shiver
with fatigue.

Passionate questions that have
no answer, keep you awake.

Laugh and have a lalapalooza of
berries. A slather of flax seeds.
Like Persephone you eat
pomegranate seeds
in a menopausal underworld,
you sense life will never be the
same.

You become proficient at self-medicating with green tea,
coffee, smoothies, mangos, poetry, yoga.
You learn it's wise to feast on every green vegetable,
believing bones won't break if you eat enough salad.
Some days, you feel unbreakable and say bring it!
Others, you need sleep, as if you haven't had any in years.
Sleep becomes the alchemy you need, as you bleed less
and dream more. There's freedom in what your body feels,
though it doesn't seem so. But if you open to the opulence of
the strange design called your life, where you hold, then let go,
you'll understand the greatest magic.

Open to the energy, over and over as a lover of life.
Sensual and zen.

A geography of joy.

A happy ending without blood
or fairytale.

Hans Christian Anderson said
"Just living is not enough, one
must have sunshine,
freedom, and a little flower."

Go through to a new world.
Bloom and make room for all
of it.

Be a biography of desire.

Feel like the sky. Fill with space
and color, heat and light.

Vast and creative.

An axis within shifts.

From menopause to zen-o-pause.

Feel beautiful and infuriating. Be
you, at last.

Know this my friend in
menopause, nothing lasts. And
you have this. Whatever it is.

It's a simple, difficult, silly minute
to fill with life and lick lilacs.
Zen-o-pause!

Wake space to power surge.
Indulge in the abundance of honest
heat, creativity, and love. Hot-flash
from the ashes like a fire goddess.

Printed in the United States
By Bookmasters